A special gift for you

_____

With love from

_____

A 3-minute forever book

EAT YOUR PEAS®

for Mom

By Cheryl Karpen

Illustrated by Sandy Fougner

Her children
rise up
and call her
blessed.

Proverbs 31:28 nkjv

At
the heart
of this little book
is a **promise**.
It's a promise from me to you
and
it goes like
this:

If you ever forget what
a wonderful mother you are
or doubt for a single moment
how grateful I am
to call you my mom...

I promise to
stop what I'm doing
and remind you
how much you mean to me.

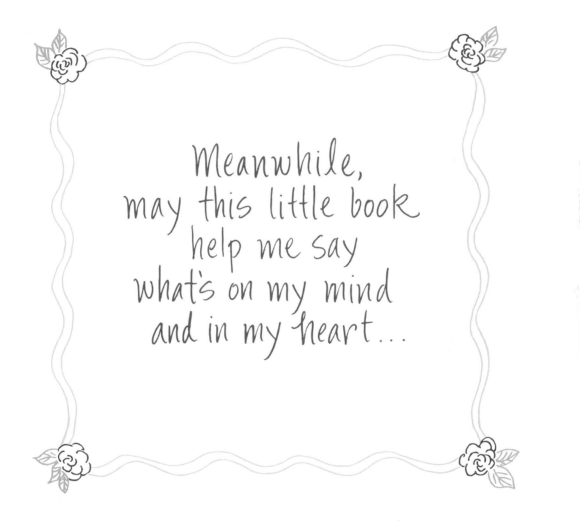

Meanwhile,
may this little book
help me say
what's on my mind
and in my heart…

Read often for maximum smiles!

I am
truly blessed
because you
are
my mother.

You: tender, loving, smart, beautiful, forgiving, strong, patient, and kind.

Me: fortunate

bumps

scrapes

bruises

Thank you
for all the tears you wiped away,
for kisses that made it better,
and your smile that said it was safe
to face the world again.

blisters

heart hurts
♡♡

scuffles

I remember
how you assured me
everything
would be okay—
even when it
felt like it was
the end of the world.
And
you were right.

You make being a mom look easy.

I know it isn't.

You have no idea
how much you taught me
when I was trying
so hard not to learn!

For all those
aggravating
years
I thought the
world revolved around
me...

I'm sorry.

I think of all the times you must have been exhausted and ready to give up, but you didn't.

May I be as strong of heart for those I love.

How did you become so wise?

(Why did it take me so long to notice?)

So much of who I am
today is because of you.

You have guided me,
nurtured me,
prayed for me,
and
loved me.

I am grateful.

You give so
unconditionally
and ask for
so little in return.

Like the loving stitches
of a quilt
you connect us
to what really matters.

Each other. Our stories.
The heart of who we are.

The older I get,
the more
you
amaze
me.

I love you.

Although I will never know
your worry or heartache,
thank you for all the times
you let me
walk my own path
and
learn in my own way.

Many
of my
personal dreams
have been
realized
because of
how you loved me
and what I learned
from you.

Thank you
for
believing in me.

Remember all the times
I took you for granted?

I never want you to feel that
way ever again.

You are so very precious to me.

What can I do to make
your life easier and better?

You
are more than
a remarkable mom.

You
are a remarkable woman.

I
will
always
need
you.

I wish you
time for yourself:

a cozy corner,

a good book,

a soak in the tub ...

You know those dreams you delayed
so the rest of us could pursue ours?
Now it's my turn to cheer you on!

Go for it

Dream
in
color

Live
large

Take a chance

You can do it!

I believe in you.

After all these years of
magnificent mothering,
let me be the one to nudge you
to do something for yourself!

Have an adventure.
Travel light.
Help yourself to seconds.
Stay out late.
Dance in the rain.
Sleep in.
Ask for what you want.
Nap in the sun.
Accept compliments.
Be silly.

Celebrate yourself...
(you deserve it!)

Embrace
your
gifts...
(You have so very many!)

Indulge yourself...
(No one deserves it more!)

And most of all, stay healthy...

Remember to always
eat your peas!

Why Peas?

She was a vibrant, dazzling young woman with a promising future. Yet, at sixteen, her world felt sad and hopeless.

Though I was living over 1800 miles away, I wanted to let this very special young person in my life know that I would be there for her, across the miles and through the darkness. I wanted her to know she could call me any time, at any hour, and I would be there for her. And I wanted to give her a piece of my heart that she could take with her anywhere—a reminder that she was loved.

Really loved.

Her name is Maddy, and she was the inspiration for my first book in the Eat Your Peas series, *Eat Your Peas for Young Adults*. At the very beginning of her book, I made a place to write in my phone number so she would know I was serious about being available. And right beside the phone number, I put my promise to listen—truly listen—whenever that call came.

Soon after the book was published, people began to ask me if I had the same promise and affirmation for adults. It was then that I realized it isn't just young people who need to be reminded of how truly special they are. We all do.

Today, Maddy is thriving and giving hope to others in her life. I like to think that, in some way, I and my book were part of helping her achieve that. If someone has given you this book, it means *you are a pretty amazing person to them*, and they wanted to let you know. Take it to heart.

Believe it, and remind yourself often.

Wishing you peas and plenty of joy,

Cheryl Karpen

P.S. My mama always said, "Eat your peas! They're good for you." The pages of this book are filled with nutrients for your heart. They're simply good for you too!

If this book has touched your life,
we'd love to hear your story.

Please send it to:
mystory@eatyourpeas.com
or mail it to:
Gently Spoken
PO Box 245
Anoka, MN 55303

With gratitude...

To my mother, Julia C. Karpen,
for being a phenomenal mother,
role model, and friend.
I wrote this book for you.

To my dear friend and illustrator, Sandy Fougner,
who is an absolute joy to collaborate with.
Her ability to make words come alive
through artful lettering and illustration is a
blessing to all who are graced by her work.

To editor, Suzanne Foust,
who is a gifted wordsmith
and PEAS treasured editor.

Other magnificent peas in the pod...
A special thank you to:
Lana Siewert-Olson,
Gina Little, Candace Abuvala,
and to my mentor, Tom Hill, for
believing in me and the power of Peas.
~CK

About the author   "Eat Your Peas"

A self-proclaimed dreamer, Cheryl
spends her time imagining and creating
between the historic river town of Anoka, Minnesota
and the seaside village of Islamorada, Florida.

An effervescent speaker, Cheryl brings inspiration,
insight, and humor to corporations,
professional organizations, and churches.
Learn more about her at www.cherylkarpen.com

About the illustrator

Sandy Fougner artfully weaves
a love for design, illustration and
interiors with being a wife
and mother of three sons.

Other books by **Cheryl Karpen**

The Eat Your Peas® Collection

now available:

Eat Your Peas® Daughter
Eat Your Peas® Faithfully

New titles sprouting up in Summer 2011

Eat Your Peas® Girlfriend
Eat Your Peas® Faithfully, Love Mom
To Let You Know I Care

Eat Your Peas® for Mom

Copyright 2011 by Cheryl Karpen

Cover design by Koechel Peterson & Associates
Minneapolis, MN

ISBN-13: 978-1-4041-8984-3

Printed in China

11 12 13 14 15 [RRD] 6 5 4 3 2

www.thomasnelson.com